ABC

Pet Care Book

Jessica Lee Anderson

AO PRESS

Paperback ISBN: 979-8-9899560-0-5

Photo Credits—Front Cover: Life on White, hikaru1222, mjf795, Nynke van Holten, Billion Photos, Hemera Technologies, Photova; Back Cover: Billion Photos (hamster fur)), Matheus Angelo, Arterogi, Life on White, Mr. Sutin Yuukrung; copyright page: Gurinaleksandr, Erin Wilkins; p. 4: Life on White, pixelshot, Jess Lessard; p. 5: hikaru1222 (cat fur), David Kenny, Stephen White, Irene Valsileskaia; p. 6: mjf795 (macaw feathers), Good Focused, Michele Jackson, victoriass88; p. 7: linephoto (fish scales), _jure, Kameleon007, Mirko_Rosenau, Dmytro Leshckenko; p. 8: 1stGallery (dog fur), Caymia, Lakshmi3, Cimmerian; p. 9: Alexas Photos (bird feathers), Sage Overoye, Gurinaleksandr; p. 10: Denis Kuvaev (parrot feathers), Ben Harding, Brad Covington, Mart Production, p. 11: Seksanwangjaisuk (potbelly pig , Schulte Productions, #Urban Photographer, Oleg Spiridonov, Kikkerdirk; P. 12: nanka-stalker (chinchilla fur), White-Plaid, Sasha Fox Walters; p. 13: tmarvin (parakeet feathers), Irina Gutyryak, Feedough, Okssi68; p. 14: Coica (cat fur), Nynke van Holten (leopard gecko & ferret), DAPA Images, memcockers; p. 15: alexis84 (cat fur), Billion Photos, Life on White (hamster & parrot), Florian Denis; p. 16: tioloco (dog fur), Jamie Casper, corners74, Visual Content; p. 17: Piya Sarutnuwat (fish scales), Nynke van Holten, Shells1, DAPA Images; p. 18: Meli1670 (parakeet feathers), Hailshadow, Billion Photos, George Doyle & Ciaran Griffin, DAPA Images; p. 19: Denista Kireva (rat fur), Anna Hirna, Brian Asmussen, PixelShot; p. 20: Deyan Georgiev (milksnake scales), Claudia Nass, SAMIphoto, Cathy Keiffer; p. 21: altanakin (fish scales), @anastas404734672, SolStock; p. 22: claraveritas (dog fur), Aleksandr Zotov, Africa Images; p. 23: ollzha (hedgehog needles), Kittisuper, Cat'chy Images; p. 24: agustavop (macaw feathers), Damedeeso, Axel Bueckert' p. 25: rottoro (dog fur), Africa Images, Byelikova Oksana; p. 26: gemredding (goldfish scales), Nick Mayorov, Andresr; p. 27: itthiPolB (dog fur), Mark Kostich; p. 28: andipantz (ball python scales), Sergei Gorin, Africa Images; p. 29: CaraMaria (dog fur), Matheus Angelo, eluxirphoto, nimis69; p. 30: Fenne, Welcomia (lizard), Erik Isselee (ball python), purple_queue , LeMusique (snake), mjf795 (macaw), Svetlanistaya, I'm Love Photography and Art, MaZiKab, Lukas (dog); p. 31: Michael Anderson, Ava Anderson

This Book Belongs to:

_____

 is for Adopt

If you and your family are thinking of getting a pet, consider adopting! Search for animal shelters or rescue centers in your area.

B is for Bedding

Bedding keeps pets comfortable. Different types of pets need different kinds of bedding.

B b

 is for Care

Care for your pets by keeping them and their homes clean. Some pets need grooming care.

C c

D is for Diet

A healthy diet is important to keep pets happy and healthy. Research what is best to feed your pet.

 is for Enrichment

Enrichment means giving animals physical and mental exercise. Pets love exploring new toys, games, activities and environments!

F is for Fees

There can be fees to adopt or buy a pet, and some places charge fees if you keep a pet in your home. It is important to consider this along with costs for medical care, food, toys, etc.

F f

G is for Gentle

Being gentle helps a pet feel safe. Treating your pet with kindness builds trust.

G g

H is for Home

Some pets need a special place to call home. They also have specific needs for a healthy home.

Hh

I is for Identification

Identification can help pets find their way home if they get lost. A collar with tags or a microchip provides information about pets.

J is for Joy

Pets are a joy to keep! Studies show that pets can lower stress and promote good health for their owners.

Jj

K is for Knowledge

Before getting a pet, it is important to have knowledge about an animal's needs and behavior. Understanding proper pet care will help your pet thrive.

Kk

L is for Laws

Depending on where you live, there may be laws in place about certain types of pets. Some local laws require licenses and have rules about leashes and more—make sure to look this up to avoid trouble.

Ll

M is for Messy

Caring for a pet can sometimes be messy! Be prepared to clean up.

N is for Name

A pet needs a name—consider one that isn't too long for your pet to recognize. Get a sense of your pet's personality to see what fits best.

O is for Observe

Use your senses to observe and learn more about your pet. What you see, hear, feel, and smell can give you important information about your pet.

P is for Patience

Owning a pet takes patience, especially if the animal behaves in a way you don't want it to. Give the pet time to settle and ask friends or family for help if you need it!

Pp

19

Q is for Quiet Time

Just like people, pets need rest and quiet time. Some pets might need more quiet time if they are sick, older, or about to shed.

Qq

 is for Responsibility

Being a pet owner is fun, but it also takes responsibility. This means you make a commitment to look after your pet and meet the pet's needs.

 is for Safety

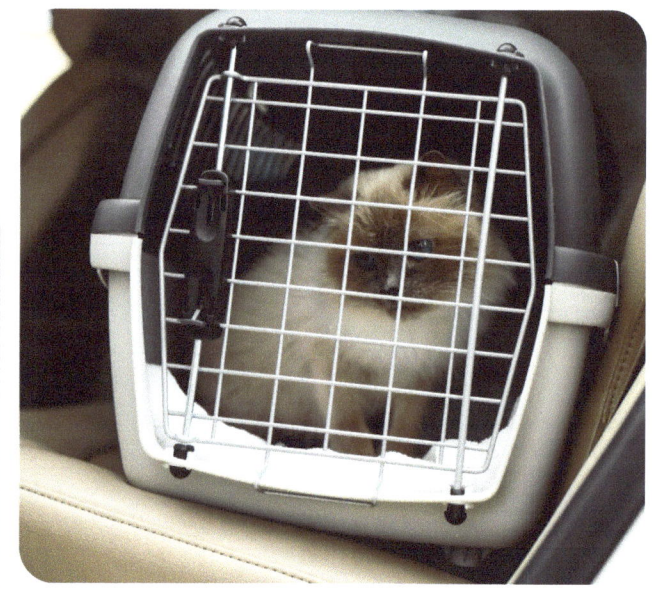

Keep your pets safe. Make sure they aren't too hot or cold, can't escape, and don't eat anything they shouldn't.

 **is for Training**

Certain pets can be trained if the rules are clear and consistent. Training can be done by rewarding good behavior with treats, praises, or playtime.

Tt

23

 is for Understanding

Learn to understand your pet's needs and personality. Create a routine to lower stress with things like mealtimes, play time, and bathroom breaks.

Uu

V is for Veterinarian

A veterinarian, or animal doctor, can help if your pet gets sick or hurt. Veterinarians work to keep pets healthy.

V v

W is for Water

Pets of all kinds need fresh water. Make sure their water container stays clean.

W w

 is for X-rays

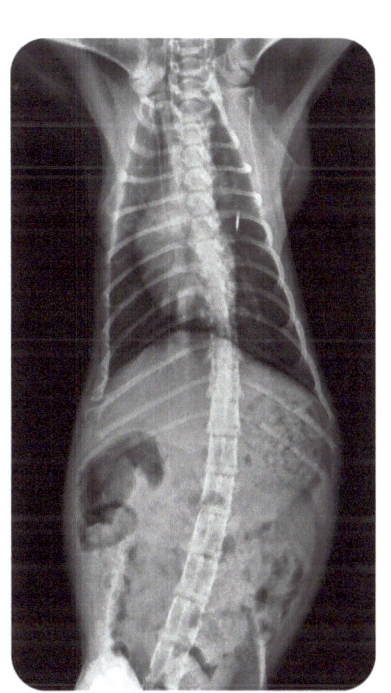 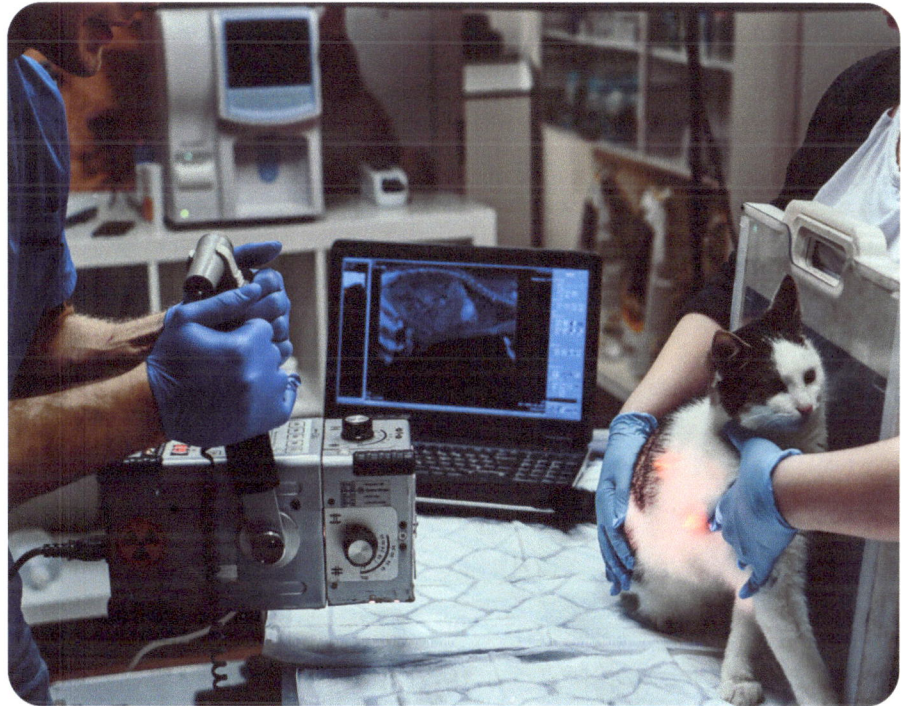

If a pet gets injured or sick, the veterinarian might order x-rays. X-rays show if a pet is sick or has any broken bones.

Xx

 is for Yucky

Pets can have potty accidents. Some pets also have yucky habits like drinking out of the toilet bowl or eating things they shouldn't.

Z is for "Zoomies"

Certain types of pets sometimes get the "zoomies"—bursts of excitement and energy! Make sure to get out of the way if your pet runs wildly so you don't collide.

5 Pet Facts

1 Dogs have a GREAT sense of smell!

 Cats spend a LOT of time sleeping.

 "WHEEK! WHEEK! WHEEK!" Guinea pigs make lots of noises.

 A "bunny binky" is the name for a rabbit's happy dance.

5 Tortoises can live for a LONG time.

Jessica Lee Anderson is an award-winning author of over 75 books for young readers. She loves pets of all kinds and cares for an elderly dog named Nike and a corn snake named Ari. Growing up, Jessica helped take care of dogs, hamsters, turtles, and a pet tarantula. She lives near Austin, Texas with her daughter, Ava, and husband, Michael. You can learn more about Jessica by visiting www.jessicaleeanderson.com.

Check out these other books in the series:

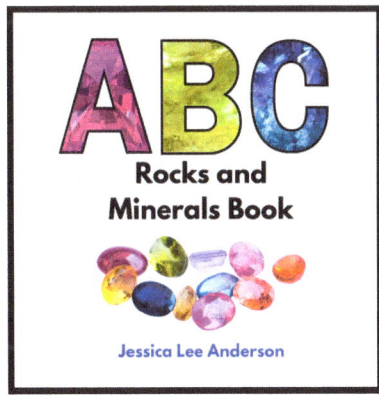